Picnic Time
by Chloe Nicole
Illustrated by Donna Catanese

Glenview, Illinois • Boston, Massachusetts • Chandler, Arizona
Upper Saddle River, New Jersey

basket

We can go on a picnic!
What can we put in the basket?

Apples are good to eat.
Apples fit in the basket.

blanket

A blanket is good to sit on.
We can take a blanket in the basket.

sandwich

Sandwiches are good to eat.
We can take sandwiches in the
basket.

Cookies can fit in the basket.
This big cake will not fit in the basket!

We can take juice in the basket.
We can drink it at the picnic.

basket

The basket is full.
We can go on a picnic!